Juicing it!

To Janos, for his sense of adventure and blissful times together

Opposite: 'Morning After' detox juice to help a hangover.
Page 4: Squeeze citrus fruits for regular doses of vitamin C.
Page 5: (top) Orange juice is great alone or as a base for other mixes;
(below left) Like other citrus fruits, tangerines contain plenty of vitamin C;
(below right) An orange tree.

THIS IS A CARLTON BOOK

This edition published in 1999

10 9 8 7 6 5 4 3 2 1

Copyright © Carlton Books Limited 1999

A CIP catalogue record for this book is available from the British Library

ISBN hardback 1 85868 823 X
ISBN paperback 1 85868 866 3

Project Editor: Martin Corteel
Project Art Direction: Brian Flynn
Production: Bob Bhamra
Picture Research: Lorna Ainger

Printed in Dubai

Juicing it!

A GOURMET'S GUIDE TO NATURAL DRINKS

Jane Pettigrew

CARLTON

Contents

A Fresh Start 6

1 Liquid Assets 8

2 The Squeeze 16

3 Fruitful Beginnings 22

4 Essential Vegetables 40

5 Juice Boosts 52

6 Creative Blends 60

Index 94

A Fresh Start

The craze for nourishing, refreshing juices surfaced in sunny Australia a few years ago, then hit America's west coast and quickly spread across the US and Canada so that most areas there now have their favourite juice bars.

In the last couple of years, Europeans have begun to recognize the appeal of healthy, colourful and fun blends and are choosing to drink customized mixes in bars, on the beach, during breaks at work and at home as an alternative to other less healthy beverages and snack foods.

Juice companies with names like Squeeze, Joose Moose, Round the Blend, Suca Juice and Crussh are opening stores in busy shopping malls and high streets in London and other European cities. And as consumers become more aware of health and the benefits of juicing, these fashionably stylish bars are attracting more and more regulars. During the early days of juice bars in America, a "new age", alternative style created a slightly faddy, hippy image, but today's youthful, colourful, trendy look makes the idea of popping in for a "smoothie" or "naked juice" much more attractively mainstream.

Alongside the change in decor has come a wider-ranging, more general concern with organic foods, safer products and healthy living, so the idea of consuming fresh products as part of a sensible diet is no longer seen as quirky or odd.

The smoke-free environment of these new outlets, the creative, adaptable juice list, and menus that include freshly made soups, great salads, and healthy low fat wraps and sandwiches are drawing in new customers every day.

And it's not just in the high street juice bar that customized blends are on offer. More and more clinics, gyms, health clubs, pharmacies, homeopathic stores, health food shops and major fashion stores are fitting the idea into the mix of services they offer.

The idea of using fresh juices as therapy against disease was established in 1938 by the German doctor Max Gerson, who claimed that our diet had a direct affect on our general health and that damaged body tissue and a build-up of toxins could be treated by regular consumption of fresh organic juices. Today, any nutrition specialist will agree that our bodies need plenty of fresh fruit and vegetables – we are regularly advised to eat at least five servings every day.

Drinks made from natural fruit and vegetable juices help replace lost energy and feed the body vital nutrients. So for anyone with a fast-paced lifestyle who has little time to shop or cook healthy food, nourishing juices can provide the answer. For breakfast, lunch, before an evening out clubbing, after a workout at the gym, between work and evening socializing, or as a quick energy boost at work, pulped fruit or whizzed-up juice is easy to digest, restores the body's balance of water and nutrition, and satisfies for much longer than other fast foods and drinks.

Use a blender to create 'smoothies' that are packed with goodness

Since all the ingredients used are fresh and prepared exactly when you want them, customized combos can be squeezed, pulped, juiced or blended to suit individual tastes. And optional add-ins such as tonic supplements or favourite herbs can add an extra kick to help fight a cold, detox after over-indulgence, perk up the concentration, or build up the body's defences against infections. What could be easier? Creating and drinking favourite juice mixes really is the best way to health and vitality.

Liquid Assets *1*

Nutritionists today know exactly what we need to eat for our bodies to stay fit and healthy. Although individual requirements vary slightly depending on age, general health and lifestyle, we should all eat a diet that gives us a balance of vitamins, minerals, proteins, carbohydrates, fats and fibre. We are what we eat. If we treat our bodies with little respect and fill them with empty calories that give high energy but low nutrition, we are more likely to develop diseases and ailments that mar or shorten our lives. If we take greater care to eat the foods that help keep the body's machinery running smoothly, we stand a far better chance of staying fit and of living longer.

One of the most important reasons for eating plenty of vitamins is the powerful *antioxidant* properties they have to protect our bodies against a long list of diseases and illnesses that includes Alzheimer's disease, cancer, cardiovascular diseases, diabetes and rheumatoid arthritis. These and other ailments are caused by the oxidation of body cells as a result of ageing, the absorption and oxidation of too much fat into the bloodstream, and the effects of 'free radicals' – the oxidants we encounter in pollution, cigarette smoke, the sun's harmful rays, industrial waste and toxins in our food. Scientists know that the oxidation process can be slowed and even reversed by eating large quantities of vitamins A, C, E and betacarotene (the precursor of vitamin A), which are powerful antioxidants.

Antioxidants are also found in *'phytochemicals'* which are not actually classified as nutrients but help to maintain our immune systems, fight infections, reduce the risk of cancer and generally keep the body healthy.

Our bodies need enzymes to digest and absorb the food we eat. In order to make those enzymes,

we need to consume certain nutrients. Many fruits and vegetables are packed full of those potent nutrients, phytochemicals and enzymes – and so they make perfect ingredients for mixed juices that are health-promoting, energy-giving, satisfying, fun to concoct and easy to make.

A good diet and exercise are vital for healthy living

To get the best from them, raw is nearly always better than cooked. More than half the nutrients in food are usually lost before it gets on to your plate. Some disappear during storage and more are destroyed by heat when the food is cooked. So the raw juice of freshly picked fruits or fresh organically grown vegetables is not just a refreshing drink – it's pure nutrition in a glass.

By pulping or juicing different combinations, you can turn the ingredients into something much more palatable and interesting than when they are eaten separately. The blended fruits and vegetables can be mixed with other ready-to-use juices, yoghurts, sorbets, dairy or non-dairy milks, soda or mineral water, honey or low-cal sweeteners to create a customized drink to suit individual tastes. And all sorts of other health-giving supplements, such as ground seeds and nuts, wheatgerm, herbal remedies and protein powders, can be added to the colourful mixtures to make sure that you get your daily dose of all the essential nutrients.

Juices are ideal as cooling drinks or energy-boosters at any time of the day, and make an ideal healthy alternative to all those high-fat, high-sugar fast foods, snacks and beverages that may give instant energy but offer very little nutrition.

The following list of crucial nutrients gives the best sources available from among the fruits, vegetables, seeds and nuts that are most suitable for juicing. Some of those dietary essentials are also found in other foods that are not listed here.

Vitamins

Our bodies need small amounts of various *vitamins* in order to function properly. Most of these come from the food and drinks we consume, although vitamin D is made by our skin's reaction to sunlight.

Table A

Vitamin	Chemical name	Essential for	A shortage can lead to	Best juice ingredients
A	retinol & betacarotene	normal growth of healthy skin and body tissue, powerful antioxidant, vision in low light	colds, infections, dry skin, mouth ulcers, acne, poor night vision	mangoes, melons, apricots papayas, tangerines, carrots, tomatoes
B1	thiamine	digestion, brain function, release of energy from carbohydrates	stomach problems, poor levels of concentration	watercress, lettuce, peppers, tomatoes
B2	riboflavin	release of energy from protein, fats & sugars, maintaining healthy skin and body tissue	dull hair & skin, eczema, dry & cracked lips	watercress, broccoli, beansprouts, tomatoes, wheatgerm, milk
B3	niacin	normal brain function, producing energy, healthy skin, digestion	headaches, depression, skin problems, insomnia, anxiety	tomatoes

Vitamin	Chemical name	Essential for	A shortage can lead to	Best juice ingredients
B5	pantothenic acid	healthy skin & hair, producing energy, brain & nerve function	muscle cramps, nausea, lack of energy	watercress, broccoli, alfalfa, tomatoes, celery, strawberries, avocados
B6	pyridoxine	digesting protein, balancing sex hormones	depression & irritability	watercress, peppers, broccoli, onions, bananas, seeds & nuts
B12	cyanocobalamin	formation of blood cells, making use of protein, nerve function	tiredness, anaemia, irritability	milk
C	ascorbic acid	fighting infection, strong bones & joints, absorption of iron, powerful antioxidant	frequent infections & colds, slow healing of cuts & bruises, skin problems	peppers, broccoli, tomatoes, watercress, lemons, limes, oranges, kiwi fruit, melons, grapefruit, pineapple, guava, mango, papaya
D	ergocalciferol cholecaliferol	strong teeth & bones	stiff & painful joints, tooth decay	(made by the body when exposed to sunlight)
E	d-alpha tocopherol	powerful antioxidant	extreme tiredness, atherosclerosis, slow healing of wounds	seeds, nuts, wheatgerm
K	phylloquinone	clotting of blood	easy bleeding	broccoli, lettuce, watercress
	Biotin	helping body use essential fats, healthy skin & hair	dry skin & hair, poor appetite	lettuce, tomatoes, grapefruit, cherries, almonds, milk
	Folic acid	brain & nerve activity, making red blood cells	anaemia, skin problems, anxiety, depression, exhaustion	spinach, broccoli, avocados, cashew nuts, peanuts, walnuts, hazelnuts, sesame seeds, wheatgerm

Minerals are needed by our bodies to help form and maintain healthy bones and teeth, for nerve and brain function and as an essential part of body tissues and fluids.

The following list gives juice ingredients that are the best source of the major minerals we need for optimum nutrition. These also exist in other foods not listed here.

Table B

Mineral	Essential for	A shortage can lead to	Best source
Calcium	a healthy heart, skin, teeth, bones, muscles, blood clotting	muscle cramps, tooth decay, arthritis, high blood pressure	parsley, prunes, brewer's yeast, almonds, pumpkin seeds
Chromium	balancing blood sugar, heart activity	irritability, drowsiness	green peppers, apples, parsnips, brewer's yeast, wheatgerm
Iron	carrying oxygen in the blood, energy	anaemia, fatigue	parsley, dates, almonds, brazil nuts, walnuts, pecan nuts, sesame seeds, pumpkin seeds
Magnesium	strong teeth & bones, healthy muscles, energy	muscle weakness, insomnia, high blood pressure, fits, depression	spinach, raisins, garlic, almonds, cashew nuts, brazil nuts, peanuts, pecan nuts, wheatgerm
Manganese	healthy bones, tissue, nerves, insulin production, reducing cell damage	dizziness, fits, painful joints	watercress, lettuce, beetroot, celery, grapes, pineapple, raspberries, strawberries, blackberries, oats
Phosphorous	bones and teeth, muscle tissue, energy production	bone fracture, muscle weakness	almost all foods
Potassium	making use of nutrients, nerves & muscles, fluid balance, secretion of insulin, heart activity, metabolism	irregular heartbeat, muscle weakness, nausea, low blood pressure, cellulite, irritability	watercress, celery, parsley, radishes, bananas

Mineral	Essential for	A shortage can lead to	Best source
Sodium	maintaining water balance, nerve activity, heart function, using energy	dizziness, low blood pressure, loss of energy nausea, headaches	beetroot, celery, watercress
Zinc	growth, healing, control of hormones, stress management, healthy nervous system, energy	infections, acne, greasy skin, depression, loss of appetite	root ginger, almonds, pecan nuts, brazil nuts, peanuts, oats

Protein is essential for the development and maintenance of healthy body tissue and to provide energy. Our main sources are milk, meat, fish, eggs, cheese, nuts and pulses, plus a small amount from vegetables.

Carbohydrates come in the form of starch (rice, pasta, bread, potatoes), sugar (fruit and vegetables) and fibre. The body digests the food and gradually releases the energy into the bloodstream along with the other nutrients contained in the food.

It is much better for our health and general well being to eat the **sugars** in fruit and vegetables than to consume the refined sugar that is found in sweets, pastries and fast foods. Refined sugar gives energy but very little nutrition.

Fat is good for you, despite what some people think, but it must be the right sort of fat – polyunsaturated. Whereas the types of fat known as saturated and monounsaturated provide energy but contain no nutrition, polyunsaturated fats protect the body against cancer, heart disease, skin disorders, tiredness and depression. The best sources for juicing and blending are seeds and nuts.

Fibre is indigestible carbohydrate and helps protect against intestinal problems and bowel disorders. The best sources are seeds, grains and raw fruit and vegetables.

Phytochemicals are thought to be as important as vitamins in protecting our bodies. They are found in many foods, including garlic, citrus fruits, berries, broccoli, cherries, grapes, papaya, melon, plums, tomatoes, green peppers, pineapple, strawberries, carrots, raspberries, radishes, alfalfa, fennel, celery and chlorophyll. It's a good idea to eat fruits and vegetables of varying colours, as each colour group contains different phytochemicals.

Select fruit, vegetables and extra ingredients carefully and the juices you make at home – or drink in the juice bar – will fill you with new energy and boost your general health.

The Squeeze 2

The equipment you need for creating juice mixes depends on what style of blends you want to create. To whiz together the flesh of fruits and vegetables – alone or with nuts, seeds, herbs and other extras – a food processor, liquidizer or blender will serve the purpose. Pulping the whole fruit or vegetable means that you lose none of the fibre, flesh or juice.

For citrus fruits you need an old-fashioned round juice squeezer or a tall chrome or stainless steel juicer with an arm that allows you to exert pressure on the fruit. Alternatively, you could opt for an electric citrus press.

To separate the juice in vegetables and fruit from the skin, core, pips and pulp you need a juice extractor attachment for your food processor or a purpose-made centrifugal juice extracting machine. For commercial use, heavy-duty juicing machines with strong motors, adjustable gear settings and hard-wearing parts serve the purpose best. These extract more juice by masticating the ingredients rather than forcing out the liquid by centrifugal force. One award-winning machine from Korea, a favourite with juice bar owners, also has bio-ceramic magnets to ionize the minerals in the extracted juice, which helps protect the nutrients by delaying oxidation.

If you are a real juice fanatic, you need all of the above, or a food processor that offers all the different functions. Then you can extract juice from some foods in the purpose-made juice machine and drink it alone – or blend it with other whole fruits, citrus juice, vegetables, ice, herbs and supplements to create a thicker, more filling drink.

Always make juices just before you drink them. Otherwise, they immediately lose some of their nutritional value.

For the blender: Prepare fruits by washing thoroughly or removing any unwanted skin or peel. Cut away any damaged or bruised flesh and

Choose whichever fruits you like, drop them into the blender and whiz

remove any core, pips, stones or seeds. Prepare vegetables by scrubbing or careful peeling and cut away any hard roots, tops or damaged pieces. Cut everything into chunks before feeding into the blender. Process with any herbs, spices, add-ins, ice cubes, etc. to make a smooth, thick drink. Try adding mineral or tap water, or ready-to-drink juices to create a thinner mix.

For the juice extractor: Wash fruit carefully, cut away any bruised or damaged flesh and remove large stones (such as those in mangoes) and any tough skin (such as on a melon). Scrub vegetables thoroughly and cut away shoots, roots and any damaged flesh. Drink the extracted juice alone or over ice, or use to blend with other fruits, vegetables, herbs, spices and add-ins.

Food Processors, Blenders and Liquidizers

When choosing a food processor or blender, you need to consider how much it holds without overflowing, how easy it is to assemble and dismantle, and how difficult it is to clean. If you are planning to use it on a daily basis, you will probably want to leave it sitting on the worktop, so choose a machine that looks good with your kitchen decor and doesn't take up too much of your available space.

Some food processors include a citrus press attachment and juice extractor. Liquidizers tend to pulverize to a finer consistency than food processors, have fewer parts to wash and take up less space.

Juice Squeezers and Citrus Presses

If you prefer an old-fashioned lemon squeezer, choose one that really does catch the pips and also allows the juice to run into a large enough container under the squeezer itself – otherwise spillages will madden you and you will waste some of the juice. If you plan to squeeze grapefruit as well as lemons, oranges and limes, choose one that is large enough to efficiently squeeze the larger fruit.

Electric citrus presses take the effort out of squeezing and should have an easy-to-use on/off switch, sensible spouts that allow juice to flow into a jug or bowl and reverse-action motor so that the flesh inside the fruit is thoroughly

A domestic juice extractor from the Magimix range

Food processors are all you need for creating pulped juices and smoothies

pressed from both directions. Some also offer a pulp selector so that you can choose how much flesh is allowed through with the juice. Look at the design features carefully before you buy in order to decide if the press suits your individual needs and expectations.

Nutritionists recommend five servings a day of dark green, root or leaf vegetables

Juice Extractors

These vary enormously in appearance, price and performance. Consider the following carefully before buying:

- Does it really separate juice from skin, pips, stones, pulp, core, etc.?
- Is it suitable for really hard fruit and vegetables?
- What percentage of juice is extracted? Most manufacturers will tell you 90%–95%, and commercial machines will squeeze out even more, leaving very dry pulp in the waste tray. Domestic extractors seem to work much better on denser fruit and vegetables such as apples, beetroot, carrots, etc. The juice from softer ingredients tends to get left behind in the pulp tray, and needs straining for further extraction.
- How much juice will it process before you have to empty out the waste?
- How easy is it to empty the waste?
- How easy is it to feed in the fruit and vegetables?
- How long will the motor run without over-heating?
- Does the heat of the motor heat the fruit and vegetables? This is undesirable as heat damages the nutrition value of the food.
- Does it have different speeds for different jobs?
- Does it feed the juice into a sealed container in the machine or directly into a glass or jug?
- Is it safe for anyone, including children, to use?

- Does it sit securely on the worktop without moving around while in use?
- Does it make a mess while operating or pouring?
- How noisy is it?
- How much space does it take up?
- How easy is it to use and dismantle?
- Is it easy to clean and can the parts go into the dishwasher?

Other necessary equipment

You will also need:

- a grain mill or grinder to pulp seeds and grains (like a coffee mill)
- a selection of sharp knives for peeling, coring, chopping and cutting
- a tough brush for scrubbing fruit and vegetables before putting through the juice extractor or blender
- a peeler that removes as thin a layer of skin as possible (if you cut away too much skin or peel, you also cut away a lot of the goodness)
- chopping boards in wood or plastic
- a sieve for straining unwanted pulp or flesh after pulping in the blender
- a grater for citrus fruits
- a nutmeg grater
- a grapefruit knife
- flexible rubber spatulas for scraping out every last drop of juice or pulped mixture from blenders and jugs

Add citrus juices to other mixes for generous doses of vitamin C

- spoons and ladles
- weighing scales
- a measuring jug

With the right equipment, easy juicing will become a way of life!

Fruitful Beginnings

3

Fresh fruits and fruit juices are invaluable because they feed us large quantities of anti-cancer vitamins A and C and vital minerals that help us stay in peak condition. They also provide energy in the form of fructose – fruit sugar – which is released slowly into the body and is much better for us than quick snacks such as chocolate and refined sugars. Nutritionists recommend five portions of fruit every day – one portion is assumed to be one whole fruit such as an apple, a pear, a peach, etc., or one cup of small fruits such as currants, berries or grapes, or one glass of pure fruit juice.

Fruits with the highest vitamin C content are citrus fruits, blackcurrants, kiwi fruit, raspberries, mangoes and papaya.

Always wash fruit before eating and, if pulping in a food processor or blender, remove any hard skin or peel and any pips and stones. If putting through a juice-extracting machine, simply wash most ingredients and put straight into the machine. Fruit and vegetables that have a thick, tough skin, though, such as melons or bananas, need to have that outer skin removed. Any large stones or pips, such as those in mangoes, need to be cut out before juicing.

Apples are thought to originate from an area between the Black and Caspian Seas. They are mentioned in the earliest writings of China, Egypt, Babylon and Greece, and charred apple remains were found in a prehistoric lake dwelling in Europe. From the days of Adam and Eve in the Garden of Eden to the seventeenth-century plantings of apple-seed in the new colonies of North America – through to relatively modern folklore that quite correctly tells us "an apple a day keeps the doctor away" – apples have always played an important part in our daily diet. They are low in

(Opposite) Tahitian woman with mango by Paul Gauguin

Apricots are rich in Vitamin A - essential for night vision

calories and contain vitamins A and C, calcium, iron, sodium and potassium – and they add dietary fibre to our diet.

Apricots are a native fruit of China where they are called "Moons of the Faithful". They are thought to have been introduced to Europe during the time of Alexander the Great and to North America by Spanish settlers. Their name derives from the Latin praecox or praecoquis meaning ripened early. Choose fruits that are dark yellow or yellow-orange (the darker they are, the richer

Blueberries have powerful antioxidant properties

the fruit in betacarotene), are fairly firm and well formed, and have a smooth, even skin. To ripen them, place in a sealed plastic bag and keep at room temperature. Apricots are a good source of dietary fibre, potassium and iron, and contain vitamins A and C.

Bananas do not grow on trees, but on plants that are part of the lily family. Their name is African, but they are thought to originate from Malaysia. They were well known in Asia, India and Africa by the sixteenth century and are said to have been taken to the New World by a Spanish missionary. Today, India grows more bananas than any other country. When bananas are ripe and ready for eating, the skin of the fruit is yellow with brown freckles. When the skin is still green, the unripe flesh contains "resistant" starch that the small intestine cannot digest. When very brown or black, the fruit can be bitter. Bananas are rich in potassium and vitamin A, and contain calcium, phosphorus, iron, and vitamins B and C. They give more than twice as much energy and three times as much protein as an apple.

Blackberries, also called brambles, grow in abundance in the hedgerows of Europe and North America and are also produced commercially. They are an excellent source of vitamin C (one serving of approximately 140 grams gives 50 per cent of the daily requirement) and fibre, and contain high levels of potassium, iron, calcium and manganese. The berries are best picked when plump, moist and glossy but not wet. Store in the refrigerator and don't ever wash the berries until just before you want to eat them because water will quickly cause them to rot.

Blackcurrants and other *Ribes* fruits (redcurrants and whitecurrants) tend to be very sour and sharp, and so need to be mixed with sweeter fruits or sweetened with honey. They have an extremely high vitamin C content – 200mg per 100 grams, which is almost four times as much as is found in oranges. The skins contain anthocyanins which are known to inhibit the development of bacteria such as E. coli.

Blueberries, native to North America, are reckoned to have a high antioxidant capacity, are full of vitamin C and a normal serving of 140 grams gives 20 per cent of the daily requirement of dietary fibre. They also contain a substance that helps guard against bacteria such as E. coli and urinary tract and bladder infections. The best ripe berries are firm and smooth and have an

Grape Harvest, Egyptian wall painting from the tomb of Nahkt, scribe and priest under Tuthmosis IV of Thebes, New Kingdom 18th Dynasty, 15th Century B.C.

The flavour of cherries blends well with other fruits in pulped juices

'Gathering Citrons'
(Old Damascus,
Jews Quarter) by
Frederic Leighton

even blue colour with a whitish bloom. Store in the refrigerator and wash just before using.

Cherries are related to the rose family and are native to Europe, North America and Asia. They were introduced to Britain by the Romans and have been growing there for almost a thousand years. In Japan certain cherry varieties have been bred for their wonderful blossoms, on trees that do not bear fruit. The fresh fruit contains vitamins A and C, along with biotin and potassium which both help to keep the skin and hair healthy. They are also believed to help flush toxins from the body and clean the kidneys.

Cranberries have a long history as both food and medicine

Cranberries are native North American fruits and were known to Native Americans as Sassamanash. Because of the vital acids that they contain, the berries are known to help keep the bladder and urinary tract healthy and so help guard against cystitis. They are also rich in vitamin C. Ready–to-use cranberry juice is useful for adding to mixes of other fruits, but, when-ever possible, choose freshly squeezed rather than concentrated varieties and use as quickly as possible after buying.

Grapefruit probably originated in Jamaica as a hybrid of the pomelo and the sweet orange and takes its name from the fact that the large globular fruit grow in clusters. The first printed record of grapefruit appeared in 1814, but it was only taken seriously as an everyday food in the early 1900s. Grapefruit come with yellow, pinkish or dark red flesh and, like all citrus fruits, are a really good source of vitamin C (half a grapefruit provides half the daily adult requirement). They also contain calcium, biotin (which helps the body to grow healthy skin and hair), vitamin A and pectin, which is thought to help reduce blood cholesterol.

Grapes have been cultivated since the beginning of civilization – Noah planted a vineyard according to the Bible; details for cultivation of the vine exist in ancient Egyptian writings; the Greeks drank wine; and the Romans planted vines in the Rhine valley in the second century AD. It is really difficult to choose sweet ripe grapes without tasting them in the shop first (so

often they look ripe and tempting and when you get them home they are sour and dry), so choose with care. When ripe, grapes are full of natural sugar and contain plenty of potassium, but offer few vitamins and minerals. But red and black grapes are excellent antioxidants.

Guavas (also called Goiaba or Guayaba) are the fruit of a plant related to the myrtle family and are thought to be native to Brazil. They are

high in vitamins, soluble fibre and pectin (good for reducing blood cholesterol), so pulp the whole lot.

Kiwi fruit originate from China and because of their green hairy appearance are also known as Chinese gooseberries. Today they are cultivated in New Zealand and California and are thought to be one of the most nutritious fruits. They are very rich in vitamin C and are one of only a few fruits

The oval Kiwi fruit is studded with hard black seeds

higher in vitamin C content than citrus fruits (weight for weight, they give five times as much as oranges) and also contain vitamins A and B. As well as being eaten fresh or in conserves, the fruit is used as a medicine against stomach upsets, diarrhoea, dysentery and skin disorders, and as an astringent and antiseptic. Choose greenish/yellow fruits that are just ripe and the flesh inside will have a yellowish, whitish or pinkish flesh, a musky odour and an acidic taste. The seeds are

that contain vitamin E – this acts as an antioxidant to protect cells from damage. They also have a high potassium content, contain calcium, are low in calories and high in dietary fibre, and can help the digestion and cleanse the system.

Lemons probably originated in north-western India, but have been cultivated in Europe, Iraq and Egypt for hundreds of years. Christopher Columbus is thought to have taken seed to Haiti on his 1493 voyage, and trees were established in

Florida in the late sixteenth century. The sharp acid taste helps to bring out the flavour of both fruits and vegetables and a squeeze of fresh juice adds an interesting tang to dull flavours. Lemons are rich in vitamin C.

Limes are closely related to lemons, but have wonderful bright green skin and flesh, are smaller, less acid and more delicate and aromatic. They are thought to have come originally from Malaysia and were reported in Europe in the thirteenth century. They have a high vitamin C content; in the eighteenth century British sailors ate limes to prevent scurvy and so acquired the nickname "limeys". The flavour of the juice marries extremely well with kiwi fruit, papaya and mango.

Lychees (also spelt litchee, lichee, liachi and leet-jee) come from China and have been a favourite fruit of the Cantonese people for hundreds of years. For the Chinese, this exotic fruit symbolizes love. When buying, choose fruits that are firm and have an even pink or red colour. They are best eaten as soon after buying as possible, but will keep for a few days in a plastic bag or sealed box in the refrigerator. To prepare, crack the skin away from the fruit and pull the white flesh away from the brown stone.

Mangoes have for a long time had connections with folklore and religious ceremonies in India – Buddha is said to have been given a mango grove as a restful place in which to sit and meditate. The name comes from the Tamil "man-kay" or "man-gay" which the Portuguese

'Orange pickers from Capri' by Leopold Robert, 1827

adopted as "manga" when they settled in western India. There are more than 500 different varieties, some more fibrous than others and each with its own particular perfume and flavour. Ripe fruit have a full fruity smell and are slightly soft when gently squeezed. If ripe, mangoes will keep well in the refrigerator for a day or two. To ripen, store at room temperature (ideally 10°–13°C) for 1–2 weeks. Mangoes have a high fibre and vitamin A content, and also contain vitamin C and calcium.

Melons were first cultivated in southern Asia or Africa and are thought to have reached China in the eighth century AD. Marco Polo (1254–1324) wrote of Afghan Turkistan: "Here grow the best melons in the world. They are cut into round slices and dried in the sun. Thus dried, they are sweeter than honey ...." The Moors encouraged cultivation of melons in Spain and from there they travelled up into northern Europe and across the Atlantic to the New World with explorers and colonizers. Melons contain quite a high proportion of sodium and a small amount of vitamins A, B and C.

Nectarines are a variety of peach but have a smooth skin. The name of this sweet, succulent, aromatic fruit is thought to date back to the seventeenth century and aptly describes its nectar-like qualities. Choose fruit that are smooth and tight and give slightly to gentle pressure. Avoid those that have very soft patches. Ripen at room temperature for a day or two, but use as quickly as possible after buying. Nectarines are sweeter

Papayas can vary in size from one to twenty pounds

than peaches and are slightly more nutritious. One whole fruit provides almost all the total daily vitamin C requirement.

Oranges come originally from the tropical regions of Asia and the name derives from

Passion Fruit are richly aromatic with a sweet and sour flavour

Sanskrit "naranga". The many varieties available today offer different levels of natural sugar and acidity, but all are extremely rich in vitamin C and also contain pectin which is thought to help reduce blood cholesterol.

Papaya (sometimes incorrectly referred to as paw paw, which is actually a custard apple) is a native of Mexico and Central America. Choose fruit with smooth, unmarked skin and press the skin gently for a soft, lightly yielding flesh inside. The fruit is very rich in vitamins A and C and contains an enzyme called papain which is used in digestive remedies. The subtle, mild sweetness of the fruit is enhanced by adding lime juice, so when mixing blended drinks with papaya, add a good squeeze of fresh lime as well.

Passion fruit comes from the Amazon and was named by Spanish missionaries who saw a resemblance between the different elements of the flower and Christ's passion – the corona is likened to the crown of thorns, the styles are the nails that held Christ to the cross, the stamens are the five wounds, and the five sepals and five petals are the 10 apostles without Judas and Peter. Ripe fruit are brown and slightly wrinkled, and inside the juicy pulp is full of little brown/black seeds. If pulping in a food processor, it is best to sieve the flesh first to remove the seeds, but when eating the fruit alone or mixing it into sauces, salad dressings or cake mixtures, use the seeds as well as the flesh. Passion fruit contain vitamins A, B and C.

Peaches come originally from China, but

Opposite: Pineapple, the Fruit of Kings

their name derives from Latin persicum malum – Persian apple! They were introduced to Europe and North America by the Spanish and were found in Mexico in the sixteenth century. They were at one time cultivated only in the gardens of the aristocracy, but became a large-scale commercial item in the nineteenth century. Ripe peaches have smooth, tight skin, but are soft to

the touch and smell sweet and perfumed. They are a good source of vitamin A.

Pears have been cultivated in Europe for about 2,000 years, having arrived there from western Asia. The gentle sweetness of their flesh blends well with more acidic fruits such as blackcurrants. They are a good source of dietary fibre, and contain small amounts of vitamins A and C. Ripe pears are soft around the stalk, and have a sweet fruity smell. Use as soon as possible after purchasing. To ripen fruit that has been bought too soon, store on a sunny window-sill.

Pineapples are sometimes known as "the Fruit of Kings" and are thought to come originally from Brazil. The fruit was brought to Spain from the West Indies by Christopher Columbus as a gift for the king and queen in 1493. A ripe pineapple can be golden or brown or yellow-brown; when choosing one, look for fresh green leaves at the crown and smell the flesh for an aromatic sweetness. Store in a cool place or in the refrigerator and use as soon as possible after buying. Pineapples contain a lot of natural sugar, and are a good source of vitamin C.

Plums originate from Asia and come in more varieties – about 2,000 – than any other stone fruit. They include damsons and greengages, which tend to be too sour for juicing or pulping, so choose instead the sweeter, juicier, yellow, red or black plums. All plums are a good source of vitamin A – which is an excellent antioxidant – and contain calcium and a small amount of vitamin C.

The Pear was introduced to the new world by the British and other Europeans

36

Pomegranates get their name from the Latin Pomum Granatum - seedy apple

Pomegranates were brought from their native Middle East to Spain by the Moors who planted an avenue of pomegranate trees in a part of the country they named Granada after the fruit. To extract the edible part, break the fruit into halves and halves again and pull out the seeds encased in their red pulp. For use in a food processor, sieve the pulp to remove the seeds, or put the red flesh and seeds through a juice extractor. Pomegranates are full of vitamin C and potassium, and also contain calcium, phosphorus, thiamine and riboflavin.

Raspberries have been cultivated since the sixteenth century and grow in most temperate climates. Their flavour is so subtle and delicious that it is best not to mix them with other strong-tasting fruits. They do blend well with peach or apricot, but the best way to bring out their flavour in a long drink is to add a little lemon or lime juice, a little sugar or honey and some mineral water. Raspberries are rich in calcium, have a high percentage of dietary fibre and contain plenty of vitamin C plus a little vitamin A. Store in the refrigerator and never wash until just before using.

Strawberries are one of summer's best-loved fruits and can add a sweet and powerful flavour to juices. They are also thought to be effective against kidney stones, gout, rheumatism and arthritis, are said to cleanse the digestive system and act as a mild tonic for the liver. When choosing fruit, look for firm berries that are an even, rich red colour and have fresh green leaves attached. Eat as soon as possible after buying as, even in the refrigerator, the berries will not last

A serving of strawberries has more Vitamin C than one orange

more than a day or two. Don't wash them until just before using. Strawberries contain a lot of natural sugar, and more vitamin C than any other berry.

Watermelons belong to the gourd family and come from Africa. Sanskrit had a word for watermelon and the fruits were depicted by artists in ancient Egypt. In 1894, Mark Twain described the watermelon as "The chief of the world's luxuries, king by grace of God over all the fruits of the earth". The seeds contain protein, zinc, vitamin E and essential fats, and can help build the body's immunity, so blend the seeds and flesh together. The flesh contains vitamins A and C and is a source of potassium and dietary fibre.

Watermelon contains no fat, no cholesterol and lots of vitamins

Essential Vegetables

4

Like fruit, vegetables are packed full of antioxidants that help our bodies fight "free radicals". The catch is that as soon as they are harvested, they begin to lose their essential nutritional value – and when they are cooked, they lose more. To get the full benefit, it is important to buy them as fresh, use them as quickly, and cook them as little as possible. Turning some of the most nutritious raw vegetables into juices is the best way to benefit from the vitamins, minerals and other elements they contain.

Buy organic whenever possible, wash just before usings and scrub or remove the minimum amount of peel if whizzing in a blender or food processor. If you are using a juice extractor, the vegetable can be used whole once it has been thoroughly scrubbed.

Alfalfa is a sprouting bean that produces fine pale green shoots. Like the mung bean that is used for beansprouts, the sprouts go on producing vitamins and minerals as the young shoot grows. As soon as a bean or seed germinates and the shoot starts to develop, the vitamin C content is multiplied by 600. Sprouting also increases the development of various B vitamins.

Avocados, natives of South America, were first known in England as "alligator pears" or "midshipman's butter". The first avocado trees were grown in California in the 1870s when trees were taken there from Mexico. Avocados contain 17 vitamins and minerals including vitamins A, B, C and E, riboflavin, iron, calcium, copper, phosphorus, zinc, niacin, magnesium and more potassium than many other fruits and vegetables. They also offer the highest protein content of any

Opposite: How does your garden grow?

fruit. Although they contain no cholesterol, they are high in calories and do contain quite a high proportion of mono-unsaturated fat, so the quantity eaten should perhaps be limited. Choose ripe avocados that are ready to use immediately by pressing the skin gently for a soft, slightly yielding flesh and avoid any brown or black discolorations. Or store unripe pears at room temperature. Once cut, stop the surface from turning brown by brushing with lemon or lime juice.

Beansprouts are usually grown from the mung bean, a native of India. The young crisp and crunchy white shoots are very low in calories and contain lots of B complex vitamins and vitamin C. Unlike other vegetables that begin to lose their vitamins as soon as they are picked, sprouting beans go on producing other nutrients so the amount of vitamin C increases. A single helping gives approximately three-quarters of the adult daily vitamin C requirement. They can be grown at home in a glass jar, or bought from supermarkets and market stalls. To grow at home, soak the beans in warm water for 10–12 hours. Drain, rinse, place in glass jars and cover with muslin, then leave in a warm, dark place and the shoots will be ready to eat in 2–6 days. It is best to store in a plastic bag or covered box in the refrigerator for up to 24 hours and wash in cold water before using.

Beetroot is thought to be a descendant of the wild beet that is found along the seacoast of the Mediterranean and along the Atlantic coast of Europe. The ancient Greeks and Romans boiled

Avocado Pears contain more potassium than bananas, peaches, raisins, carrots and broccoli

43

the leaves, which have a similar flavour and food value to spinach and can be juiced or cooked and eaten in the same way. The roots have the highest sugar content of any vegetable and are a good source of vitamins and minerals including vitamin C, manganese and sodium. Best are the small, young summer beets that give a deliciously sweet juice – it cleanses the system and gives mixed juices a fabulous deep red colour. For use in domestic juice extractors, cut off the skin before juicing. For use in heavier-duty machines, just scrub clean before juicing.

Broccoli originated about 2,500 years ago from the wild cabbage of coastal Europe and the varieties we grow today have developed from the domesticated forms of the plant grown in Italy about 2,000 years ago. The name derives from the Latin "bracchium" meaning "branch". There are several different varieties that come in green, purple, and dark blue-green, and the Italians have been cultivating the variety known as calabrese in the province of Calabria since the sixteenth or seventeenth century. Choose heads that are tight and firm and a good fresh colour, then use as soon as possible after picking or buying. If storing in the refrigerator, wrap loosely in plastic film or in a plastic bag. Before using, wash thoroughly and trim off any very coarse stalks. Broccoli is an excellent source of vitamins A, B and C (one portion of approximately 100 grams gives over half the daily requirement) and has a powerful antioxidant effect.

One carrot a day is enough to help maintain good night vision

Carrots are thought to originate from Afghanistan. Choose organic whenever possible and, for pulping in a food processor or blender, use young, tender carrots that have been scrubbed or scraped. Put through a juice extractor, fresh carrots will give an excellent sweet juice that combines well with spinach, apples, radishes, beetroot, parsnip, and other root and leaf

45

Homeopathic remedies for headaches and nervous tension often include celery roots and seeds

vegetables. Carrots have an extremely high vitamin A content (more than a hundred times that of courgettes or tomatoes) and provide vitamin C, calcium and sodium.

Celery is a native of the Mediterranean and Middle East. It was used as a flavouring by the ancient Greeks and Romans and as a medicine by the ancient Chinese. In other ancient writings it is mentioned as a medicinal herb and has for many years been regarded as an aphrodisiac. It is a member of the carrot family and is related to the parsnip and to parsley. The earliest record of its cultivation is in France in the early seventeenth century. Choose fresh, crisp heads and store loosely wrapped in plastic film or in a covered container in the refrigerator. Use as soon as possible after buying and wash thoroughly before putting through the juicer. Celery is very low in calories, has a high potassium content, gives vitamins A and C and may help to lower blood cholesterol levels and blood pressure. Use the leaves as well as the stalks for maximum food value.

Cucumbers come from the same family as courgettes, pumpkins, marrows, watermelons and squashes. They are thought to come originally from India and have been cultivated for around 3,000 years. They have little nutritional value but a high water content, so when added to juices they help to maintain the necessary levels of body fluids. Choose any variety, but buy cucumbers that are firm, unwrinkled and evenly coloured. They will keep well in the refrigerator for a few days.

Fennel is a native of southern Europe and is sometimes known as Florence fennel or sweet fennel. Every part of the plant is useful – the bulb for juicing or as a raw salad vegetable; or steamed, roasted, braised or stir-fried; the leaves for chopping into salads or for garnishing; the seeds to aid the digestion. It is also thought to have aphrodisiac properties. It is low in calories and is a good source of betacarotene – the plant form of vitamin A and an excellent antioxidant.

Garlic is closely related to the onion and is regarded by some as a miracle food that can help protect the body against asthma, arthritis, viruses, bacteria, colds, nasal congestion, heart and artery diseases and high blood pressure. It is also used to treat impotence. It comes originally from Central Asia, but is now grown all around the world. It is the sulphur compounds in garlic that provide its health-giving properties and many

people believe that it is better eaten raw, since cooking destroys many of its volatile elements. The recommended daily dose is 1–2 small cloves.

Kale (also known as curly kale or borecole), a type of cabbage, is a native of Britain and the eastern areas of the Mediterranean. In 100 grams there are more than three-quarters of the daily recommended intake of vitamin A and almost

The Ancient Egyptians used garlic to cure headaches, heart disorders and intestinal complaints

Add the juice of the parsnip to mixed vegetable blends for sweetness and energy

Onions were regarded by the Egyptians as a symbol of the universe and their name may come from the Latin "unus" meaning "one". Like garlic, they have a long history of use as a cure-all. Eaten raw, they are thought to ward off colds, reduce blood cholesterol, protect against heart disease and help the circulation. Because of their sulphur compounds, they may also be helpful against cancer. Add a few spring onions, a couple of shallots or half a small onion to vegetable juice mixes.

Parsnips are at their best after the first frosts of winter because, with exposure to the cold, the high starch content starts to turn into sugar and so the flavour is sweeter and fuller. Choose smaller roots that are firm and clean. Parsnips are a good source of vitamins C and E and of dietary fibre.

Peppers (also known as sweet peppers and capsicums) come in four colours – green, yellow, orange and red. The green pepper ripens to one of the other three colours, becoming sweeter as it

twice the required amount of vitamin C. It also gives iron and calcium and is a powerful antioxidant. It's a good idea to combine it with tomatoes and peppers or other fruit and vegetables that are rich in vitamin C because the vitamin helps the body to absorb iron.

Lettuces come in many different shapes and forms and are said to originate in the Mediterranean. They are all very low in calories and the nutritional content varies according to type, season and freshness. Most contain vitamin C, betacarotene, calcium and iron. The darker outside leaves contain more betacarotene – the plant form of vitamin A – than the paler inside leaves, so use plenty of the outer layers.

Onion juice is thought to help cure many common ailments

48

The Chinese use red peppers as a tonic for the heart, stomach and circulation

does so. Weight for weight, green peppers contain twice as much vitamin C as oranges, and red peppers three times as much. They are also a good source of betacarotene. Choose firm, plump peppers and look and feel them over carefully for bruises and breaks in the skin.

Radishes come originally from Asia and Europe and get their name from the Latin "radix", meaning "root". They are related to the mustard plant, which explains their hot, peppery flavour. They are available in several shapes and sizes – small and round, olive-shaped, turnip-

shaped, elongated – and although the most common are red or pink, some are white or yellow. Mooli, a long white root, is closely related, and

Radishes are used in herbal medicines for digestive disorders

One medium tomato contains 40% of the recommended daily intake of vitamin C

has the same crisp, peppery quality. Radishes contain small amounts of vitamin C and calcium.

Rocket grows wild in many parts of Europe. It is related to the mustard plant and the leaves have a deliciously peppery, spicy flavour. Like all green leaf vegetables, rocket is a good source of vitamin C, vitamin B1 (thiamine) and biotin which helps to keep the skin, hair and nerves healthy.

Spinach was cultivated by the Greeks and the Romans and arrived in Northern Europe some time in the sixteenth century. It became more popular in the 1920s and is today considered a valuable salad leaf when eaten raw. Some people believe that it is full of iron, though in fact it is not an especially good source of the mineral. However, it does contain plenty of vitamin C and betacarotene, and is thought to help guard against cancer because it contains lutein, which is a carotenoid pigment that has powerful antioxidant effects. It is recommended to stave off high blood pressure and anaemia.

Tomatoes (once called apples of paradise) are

the fruit of a plant that is a member of the night-shade family. It is likely that the wild species originated in the South American Andes – probably mainly Peru and Ecuador. Tomatoes are thought to have been cultivated first in Mexico and their name comes from the Aztec word "tomatl". The French called them 'pommes d'amour' because they were believed to have aphrodisiac powers, while the Italians knew them as 'pomodoro' which indicates that the early ones were yellow or golden. They were also called 'pommes des Mours' because it is said they were a favourite vegetable of the Arabs. The Italian and French names may in fact be a corrupted version of that name. When tomatoes were first introduced to Europe, people were suspicious because of their relation to Belladonna – deadly nightshade – and in fact the roots and leaves are poisonous. Tomatoes are full of vitamins A, C and E, and contain potassium and lycopene, which is a carotenoid that may help protect against cancer.

Watercress, a member of the mustard family, is a native of Europe and North America. It grows wild floating in rivers and streams or on mud and is today cultivated in many countries. It is a natural antibiotic, helps the body to expel toxins, relieves upset stomachs, is good for the kidneys and liver, helps keep the urinary tract healthy and is an excellent source of vitamin C and betacarotene. Choose bunches or bags that are crisp and dark green, and use as quickly as possible as the leaves quickly start to deteriorate and turn yellow.

Watercress is rich in vitamin C and so has the alternative name 'scurvy grass'

Juice Boosts 5

The wonderful thing about mixing juices is that all sorts of other nutrients can be added in the form of ground nuts, dried fruits, herbs, spices, protein powders and health-giving natural substances such as ginseng and spirulina. The last of these is a concentrated vegetable supplement that is power-packed with antioxidants, vitamins, minerals, organic protein and omega 3 and 6 – the oils that our bodies need to maintain the immune system and keep our blood vessels, joints and skin healthy.

All those extras can be measured into a blend to suit individual health needs so that each time you blend raw fruit or vegetables with a chosen supplement, you really are creating a meal in a glass.

Nuts, Seeds and Grains

Most nuts and seeds are an excellent source of protein, minerals and the healthy polyunsaturated fats that we need to guard against cancer, heart disease, skin problems, allergies and infections. The most useful nuts are almonds, cashews, brazil nuts, walnuts and pecans. Sesame and sunflower seeds are especially rich in vitamin E, calcium, zinc, and linoleic acid, which helps to keep cell membranes healthy. Pumpkin seeds are full of iron, magnesium and zinc. Walnuts and pumpkin seeds are also thought to have aphrodisiac properties.

Some seeds contain toxins which make them difficult to digest – so before using, roast or toast them by tossing in a dry pan until they begin to turn lightly brown.

Opposite Picture: Honey bee

Grains give protein, carbohydrate, fibre, iron and other nutrients to our diet. When grains are refined for modern use in breads, the germ and bran are removed, which means that all the B and E vitamins and some of the minerals are lost. Wheatgerm puts back into our diet vitamin B2 (riboflavin), vitamin E, folic acid and magnesium. Oats and oatmeal give carbohydrates and proteins, a little fat and plenty of fibre.

Spices and Herbs

A pinch of a favourite spice adds an extra interest to fruit and vegetable juices. Experiment to find the flavours that work best for you. The most useful are ground cloves, cinnamon, nutmeg, mace and ginger.

As well as adding flavour, fresh herbs add their own health benefits to juices. Use them when they

Basil, the natural tranquiliser

are as fresh as possible, picked straight from the garden or very soon after buying.

Anise has a liquorice taste and is said to be good for the digestion and for coughs and breathing problems.

Basil is a natural tranquillizer – it calms the nervous system. It is also thought to relieve headaches and nausea.

Chilli contain vitamin C and may help against breathing problems. Be very careful how much you add – their fiery nature can spoil and overwhelm other flavours and set your mouth burning, but a little adds interest to otherwise dull flavours.

Chives stimulate the appetite and aid the diges-

Anise, whose leaves, stalks and seeds can act against indigestion

tion. They give a slightly oniony flavour to vegetable juices.

Coriander leaves have a pungency that blends well with spinach, celery, cucumber and coconut. It is thought to be useful as a tonic for the heart and the stomach. Coriander seeds help guard against urinary infections.

Dandelion is said to help prevent stomach aches and high blood pressure and may be helpful in the treatment of breast cancer.

Dill can help to treat indigestion, stomach aches, coughs and colds.

Fennel can help against indigestion, nausea, insomnia and impotence. Use the feathery leaves or the seeds.

Ginger root is prescribed for indigestion, hangovers, coughs and colds, sinus problems and nausea, and helps the digestion of fatty foods. It is also thought to be a potent aphrodisiac.

Lemon balm (melissa) gives a wonderful citrus flavour and is thought to be good for migraines, coughs, toothache, indigestion and asthma.

Mint adds a zing to juices made with salad leaves, cucumber, citrus fruits, melon and pineapple. It has all sorts of benefits including alleviating stomach cramps and indigestion, nausea and travel sickness.

Nettle leaves contain vitamins A and C, potassium and fibre. They help to treat anaemia, asthma, kidney problems, arthritis, rheumatism and diarrhoea.

Parsley is rich in vitamins A and C, iron, calci-

Red Chilli, use very sparingly to add a tang to juices

um and potassium. It freshens the breath and can help against allergies.

Rosemary is useful for treating indigestion, arthritis and circulatory problems. Use sparingly, as its flavour can be overpowering and too much may be toxic.

Thyme is an antiseptic and helps treat the effects of colds and indigestion. Its sweet, aromatic flavour goes well with all vegetables.

Homeopathic "Superfoods"

Juice bars generally offer a list of homeopathic supplements that can be added to the blends to suit each customer's health needs. They are available from chemists, health food and homeopathic stores and so can be easily bought for home use. The following are the most commonly offered.

Acidophilus adds "friendly" bacteria to the digestive system to help fight intestinal infections. It is also thought to lower blood cholesterol.

Barleygrass provides all the nutrients the body needs, including concentrated chlorophyll. Like wheatgrass, it is usually taken as a 1- or 2-ounce shot. As juicing it demands a special machine, it's best to consume barleygrass in a juice bar.

Bee pollen contains enzymes, vitamins, hormones and amino acids and is thought to be helpful in treating allergies, indigestion, sore throat, skin disorders and fatigue.

Brahmi is a bitter herb used to relieve stress, sinus problems and insomnia.

Brewer's yeast is a source of protein and B-complex vitamins.

Damiana treats depression, coughs and nasal congestion.

Echinacea is a natural antitoxin and antiseptic, boosts the immune system, promotes healing and is helpful for the circulation and respiration.

Gingko is an aid to digestion, helps against allergies and is used to treat tuberculosis, other breathing illnesses, kidney problems and impotence.

Bee pollen is thought by some to be a nutrionally perfect food

Opposite: Rosemary, an aromatic herb

Ginseng is credited with many health-giving properties including strengthening the immune system, purifying the blood, lowering blood cholesterol, stimulating digestion, preventing cell damage, increasing stamina – and with relieving stress, rheumatism, sciatica, tiredness, asthma, nervous disorders, coughs and colds.

Grapefruit seed extract has antibiotic, antiseptic, antibacterial and disinfectant properties. Helps treat candida and throat infections.

Protein powders help ensure that the body takes in as much protein as it needs for energy and for the development and maintenance of body tissues.

Spirulina, an algae, is a concentrated organic vegetable nutrient that is high in protein and loaded with vitamins, minerals and antioxidants. It is said to be the richest whole-food source of vitamin B12 and is 25 times richer in betacarotene than carrots.

Wheatgrass is grown from the red wheat berry and is a source of concentrated chlorophyll, enzymes, vitamins and minerals. It is thought to

Dried figs are rich in calcium and provide energy in the form of sugar

purify the blood, fight bacteria, improve digestion, reduce high blood pressure, reduce the risk of cancer, help prevent tooth decay, improve healing and neutralize toxins in the body. Like barleygrass, juicing it needs a special machine, so drink a daily 1- or 2-ounce shot at your local juice bar.

Other Optional Extras

Dried fruits provide energy in the form of sugar and are rich in fibre. Add raisins, sultanas, figs, dates and prunes for iron and calcium, and prunes and dried apricots for betacarotene.

Honey gives energy, but contains fewer calories than sugar. It is thought to have antiseptic, decongestant, sedative and aphrodisiac properties.

Yoghurts contain vitamins B2 and B12, calcium and phosphorus. Live yoghurts are best as they protect the digestive system against infections and bacterial imbalance.

Mineral and soda water – we need to drink between 1.5 and 2 litres of water a day to keep kidneys healthy and cleanse the body of unwanted toxins. Bottled mineral waters do not necessarily contain more or better minerals than tap water and can be too high in sodium. Check labels for contents.

Ready-to-drink juices, such as apple, tomato, grape and orange, and coconut milk provide an easy addition that thins and flavours home-juiced blends. But they are never as high in nutrients as freshly squeezed or pulped fruit and vegetables because the food value quickly reduces during storage. Whenever possible, use the fresh product.

Dried Rasins add sweetness, iron and fibre to pulped juices

59

Creative Blends

Concocting juices is flexible and fun. There are no hard and fast rules except that they should taste good and suit individual preferences and dietary needs. The following are ideas and guidelines that can be adjusted or adapted to suit your favourite flavours and ingredients.

Naked Juice

This first section requires the use of a juice-extracting machine to make refined juices with no pulp or additions – except perhaps a little seasoning where liked. Juices made like this are extremely easy for the body to absorb and digest, and give you a concentration of pure nutrition.

Blends made with vegetables sometimes need the addition of apples, pears or other fruits for sweetness. Mix and match to sit yourself. Most savoury blends do not need further seasoning, but a little salt and/or freshly ground black pepper can be added to taste. Sweet mixes can be sweetened if necessary with a little honey.

These recipes give sufficient quantities for one glass of each mix. Serve at room temperature or over ice, or add mineral water, soda water or other ready-to-drink juices to make thinner drinks that go further and are more thirst quenching.

Opposite Picture: 'Beet it'

Apple Zinger

Apple Zinger

The fresh ginger helps the digestion and adds a tang to a mix that delivers vitamin A – important for night vision – and vitamin C.

1 large apple
3 carrots
1.25cm (½ inch) piece of root ginger
1 orange

Wash the apple and cut into chunks. Scrub the carrots, discard the tops and cut the carrots into chunks. Cut the skin from the ginger and cut into smaller pieces. Juice the orange by hand or in an electric citrus press. Feed the apple, carrots and ginger into the juicer, then mix with the freshly squeezed orange juice.

Beet It

This is an intense mix of antioxidants and, although the spinach contains less iron than most people think, it does deliver a small quantity of the mineral, while the parsley adds more.

a large handful of spinach leaves
1 small beetroot
2 carrots
a small handful of fresh parsley

Wash the spinach thoroughly. Peel the beetroot very thinly, cut off any root and cut the flesh into chunks. Scrub the carrot, cut off the top and cut the flesh into chunks. Wash the parsley and break up into small pieces. Roll up the spinach leaves tightly and feed with the other vegetables and the parsley into the juicer.

Crimson Cleanser

Beetroot and watercress together help clear the system of toxins and make a juice that is full of minerals as well as vitamins. The beetroot's naturally high sugar content gives a powerful sweetness to any juice blend.

1 medium beetroot
1 apple
a large handful of watercress
the juice of ¹/₂ a lime

Thinly peel the beetroot, cut off any root and cut the flesh into chunks. Wash the apple and cut into chunks. Wash the watercress. Feed all the vegetables into the juicer. Squeeze the juice of the lime by hand or in a citrus press and add to the vegetable juices. Stir well.

Crimson Cleanser

Roots

The carbohydrate content of the parsnips and carrots gives energy, while the cucumber thins the juice with its natural water content and gives the body the fluids it needs.

1 large parsnip
2 carrots
¹/₂ a cucumber
a pinch of mild curry powder

Scrub the parsnip and carrots, cut off their tops and cut the vegetables into chunks. Wash the cucumber and cut into chunks. Feed the vegetables into the juicer, add the curry powder to the extracted juices and mix well.

The Curl

Although juicing removes the dietary fibre we only get by eating the whole food, the concentration of vitamins A and C in the curly kale and the celery makes this a really nourishing mix.

3–4 curly kale leaves (kale gives a very concentrated-flavour, so use sparingly)
4 radishes
2 sticks of celery
1 apple
¹/₄ clove of garlic

Wash the kale leaves thoroughly. Scrub the radishes and cut off the tops. Scrub the sticks of celery and cut into chunks. Wash the apple and cut into pieces. Peel the garlic clove. Roll up the kale leaves tightly and feed with the other ingredients into the juicer. Mix together the extracted juice and serve.

Vitamix

Broccoli, full of vitamins A, B and C, is one of the most powerful antioxidants and its flavour blends well with the sweetness of the red pepper.

50g (2oz) broccoli
½ a cucumber
½ a red pepper
1–2 small spring onions
a pinch of freshly grated nutmeg

Wash the broccoli and the cucumber. Wash and deseed the red pepper and cut into pieces. Peel the spring onions and cut off the roots. Feed the vegetables into the juicer, add the nutmeg to the extracted juice and mix well.

Iron Rations

The avocado, spinach and parsley all contribute iron to this blend, along with a good mix of other essential minerals.

a handful of spinach
a handful of fresh parsley
2 carrots
1 avocado
a squeeze of lemon juice
a little salt and freshly ground black pepper

Wash the spinach and parsley. Scrub the carrots, cut off the tops and cut the flesh into chunks. Peel the avocado, remove the stone and cut the flesh into pieces. Roll the spinach leaves up tight and feed into the juicer with the other ingredients. Season and mix well.

Iron Rations

Red Devil

Red Devil

Tomatoes are a powerful force against cancer and deliver more vitamin C than orange juice. The radishes in this mix can help the digestion and the red pepper adds more vitamins A and C.

4–5 tomatoes
5–6 radishes
1 red pepper
a small pinch of chilli powder

Wash the tomatoes, remove the stalks and cut into pieces. Scrub the radishes and cut off the tops. Wash and deseed the red pepper and cut into chunks. Feed all the vegetables into the juicer. Mix the juice with the chilli powder and stir well. Serve at room temperature or over ice.

C Blast

Fight off colds with this juice rich in vitamin C. Add a little honey if required to give a hint of sweetness.

1 lemon
2 oranges
3 kiwi fruits
2 guavas

Squeeze the juice from the lemon and oranges by hand or in an electric citrus press. Cut a thin layer of skin from the kiwi fruit and cut into pieces. Cut the skin from the guavas and cut the fruit into pieces. Feed the kiwi fruit and guava into the juicer. Mix the extracted juice with the lemon and orange juice.

Salad Days

Use the beansprouts absolutely fresh and they will be full of B complex vitamins and vitamin C. The spinach and fennel add vitamins A and C.

50g (2oz) beansprouts or alfalfa
½ a cucumber
a large handful of spinach leaves
a head of fennel

Wash the beansprouts or alfalfa.
Wash the cucumber and cut into pieces.
Wash the spinach thoroughly.
Cut away any discoloured parts of the fennel and cut into chunks.
Roll up the spinach tightly and feed into the juicer with the other ingredients.
Mix the extracted juice thoroughly.

Passion Juice

For centuries, fennel and celery have both been recognised as powerful sexual stimulants. Add ginger to increase desire and garlic to arouse the senses and you have a potent aphrodisiac.

1 apple
a small head of fennel
½ a cucumber
3 sticks of celery
1.25cm (½ inch) piece root ginger
½ clove of garlic

Wash the apple and cut into pieces.
Wash the fennel, cut away any brown parts and cut into chunks.
Wash the cucumber and cut into pieces.
Scrub the celery and cut into pieces.
Cut the skin from the ginger and peel the clove of garlic.
Feed all the ingredients through the juicer.

Salad Days   Mix the extracted juice thoroughly.

A New Leaf

Full of vitamins and minerals, this blend gets its tang from the spring onion and a light sweetness from the pear.

6 lettuce leaves (iceberg or round lettuce)
2 spring onions
4 radishes
1 stick celery
1 pear

Wash the lettuce leaves thoroughly. Wash the spring onions, cut off the roots and remove the outer leaves. Scrub the radishes and cut off the tops. Scrub the celery and cut into chunks. Wash the pear and cut into pieces. Roll the lettuce leaves up tight and feed with the other ingredients into the juicer. Blend the extracted juice thoroughly.

Peach Dream

This beautiful pink mix is full of vitamin A from the peaches and pear, and vitamin C from the pomegranate, pear and lime juice.

2 pomegranates
1 pear
2 peaches
a squeeze of lime juice

Break the pomegranates into quarters and pull out the red pulp and seeds. Wash the pear and cut into pieces. Wash the peaches, remove the stones and cut the flesh into pieces. Feed all the ingredients into the juicer. Add the squeeze of lime juice to the extracted juice and mix well.

A New Leaf

Opposite picture:
C–Blast

Tropical Tang

These fruits from sunny places give masses of vitamins. The papaya's natural enzyme, papain, helps the digestion.

½ a papaya
2 × 1.25cm (½ inch) slices of fresh pineapple
75–100g (3–4oz) grapes
2–3 fresh mint leaves
juice of ½ a lime

Cut the skin carefully from the papaya and cut the flesh into chunks. Remove the skin from the pineapple and cut the flesh into chunks or strips. Wash the grapes. Squeeze the juice from the lime by hand or in an electric citrus press. Put the papaya, pineapple, grapes and mint through the juicer, add the lime juice to the extracted juices, mix well and serve.

Pink Perfection

If preferred, this mix can be made in a blender (after peeling and coring the pear and skinning the melon) to get the full benefit from the fibre and all the protein, minerals and essential oils in the watermelon seeds.

1 pear
175–225g (6–8oz) chunk of watermelon
50g (2oz) raspberries
a pinch of ground cinnamon

Wash the pear and cut into pieces. Cut the rind from the watermelon and cut the flesh into chunks. Pick over or rinse the raspberries. Feed the fruits into the juice extractor. Add the cinnamon to the extracted juices and mix well.

Smoothies

Smoothies are made from whole fruits and vegetables which are whizzed in the blender or food processor with milk, water, juice, sorbet or ice cream. If you freeze fruit before you blend, the mix will be thicker and smoother. Or, if you don't like your drinks really cold, leave out the ice and use the ingredients at room temperature. Add spices, herbs and sweeteners to suit your taste, then drink through a straw from a tall glass.

To make the following smoothies, you need a citrus press, a blender or food processor – and a grain mill if you want to add pounded seeds and grains to the mixtures.

Above: Cranberry Cooler, Opposite: Tangy Avocado

Orchard Cream

Dairy Smoothies

Use semi-skimmed or skimmed milk, live yoghurt, fromage frais or crème fraîche to whisk up thick, satisfying shakes. In most of the blends, the balance of ingredients can vary to suit individual taste and seasonal availability of fruits. The nutrient value will change slightly, but the concoction will still contain an extremely nourishing, healthy drink that is almost a meal in itself.

Go Bananas

The banana's carbohydrate content and the natural sugar in the strawberries make this a perfect drink before or after a workout at the gym or to give energy for any other demanding physical activity.

1 banana
50–75g (2–3oz) strawberries
2 tablespoons live natural yoghurt
3–4 teaspoons honey (or more to taste)
3–4 ice cubes

Peel the banana and cut into chunks. Hull and wash the strawberries. Put all the ingredients into the blender or food processor and whiz until smooth and well mixed and all the ice is crushed. Serve in a tall glass.

Peach Latte

This is a delicious exotically sweet mix. For a thinner blend, use skimmed milk or mineral water.

75–100ml (3–4fl oz) semi-skimmed milk
½ a papaya
1 × 1.25cm (½ inch) slice of pineapple
2 peaches
3–4 ice cubes
juice of ½ a lime

Cut the skin thinly from the papaya and remove the seeds. Cut the flesh into pieces. Cut away any skin or eyes from the pineapple and cut the flesh into chunks. Wash the peaches (or remove the skin), cut in half and remove the stones. Put all the ingredients into the blender and whiz until smooth. Serve in a tall glass.

Go Bananas

The Big Breakfast

The Big Breakfast

Start your day with concentrated fruit sugar for energy, essential fats for healthy skin and hair, and a good dose of vitamins and fibre.

3–4 ready-to-eat prunes
3–4 pecan nuts
1 apple
2–3 oranges
2 tablespoons live natural yoghurt
a little honey, if required

Cut the prunes open and remove the stones. Peel the apple very thinly, and cut away the stalk and core. Cut the flesh into chunks. Juice the oranges by hand or in a citrus press. Put all the ingredients into the blender and whiz until smooth.

Banango

Seeds deliver a valuable quantity of the polyun-saturated fats we need for protection against heart disease and can be added to any blend.

1 banana
1 small or ½ a large mango
1 dessertspoon toasted sunflower seeds
1 dessertspoon toasted pumpkin seeds
75-100ml (3-4 fl oz) semi-skimmed milk
3–4 ice cubes
a little honey

Peel the banana and cut the flesh into chunks. Thinly peel the mango and cut the flesh away from the stone. Put the seeds through the electric grinder. Put all the ingredients into the blender and whiz until smooth.

Orchard Cream

Orchard fruits combine to give vitamins A and C. Add the spice to lift the naturally light flavours.

3 plums
1 pear
a pinch of ground cinnamon
3–4 teaspoons honey
3–4 ice cubes
75–100ml (3–4fl oz) semi-skimmed milk

Wash the plums, cut in half and remove the stones. Thinly peel the pear, cut away the stalk and core. Cut into chunks. Place all the ingredients in the blender and whiz until smooth.

Tangy Avocado

The smooth richness of the avocado combines well with the sharp tang of the tomatoes and the zing of the lime juice.

1 avocado
3 tomatoes
¼ cucumber
2 tablespoons live natural yoghurt
juice of 1 small lime
salt and pepper
a pinch of chilli powder

Peel the avocado, remove the stone and cut the flesh into chunks. Cut the tomatoes into quarters and cut away the hard core. Peel the cucumber and cut the flesh into chunks. Put all the ingredients into the blender and whiz until smooth.

Non-dairy smoothies

Replace milk and yoghurt with soy milk, rice milk, coconut milk, sorbets, mineral water, soda water and other ready-to-drink juices to concoct dairy-free shakes.

Berry Shake

Berry Shake

The skin of the blueberries contains masses of goodness so the fruits are best blended rather than juiced. Whizzed with other summer berries, they make a delicious thick shake.

50g (2oz) blueberries
50–75g (2–3oz) strawberries
1 apple
75–100ml (3–4fl oz) soy milk
3–4 cubes of ice

Wash the blueberries and remove any stalks. Hull and wash the strawberries. Peel and core the apple and cut into chunks. Put all the ingredients into the blender and whiz until smooth.

Citrus Sensation

This blend contains a concentration of Vitamin C and so is perfect for fighting off infections such as colds and flu.

1 grapefruit
2 oranges
1 apple
100ml (4fl oz) sparkling mineral water
2 mint leaves
4 teaspoons honey (more or less to taste)

Juice the grapefruit and oranges by hand or in a citrus press. Peel and core the apple and cut into pieces. Wash the mint leaves. Put all the ingredients into the blender and whiz until smooth.

Pink Passion

If you don't have any passion fruit sorbet, use the fruit itself and add a little sugar or honey to sweeten the mix.

100g (4oz) raspberries
1 banana
2 scoops of passion fruit sorbet
3–4 cubes of ice

Pick over or rinse the raspberries. Peel the banana and cut into chunks. Place all the ingredients in the blender and whiz until smooth and pink.

Cranberry Cooler

Cranberry juice is invaluable in keeping away problems such as cystitis. Its sharpness blends well with ripe pear and any type of sweet melon.

1 pear
100g (4oz) melon (honeydew or other sweet variety)
75–100ml (3–4fl oz) ready-to-use cranberry juice
3–4 teaspoons honey (or more to taste)
a pinch of ground cloves
3–4 cubes of ice

Wash the pear and cut into pieces. Cut the skin from the melon, remove the seeds and cut the flesh into chunks. Put all the ingredients into the blender and whiz until smooth.

77

Kiwi Krush

Summer Fizz

Because bananas and mangoes are so dense in texture, they give a very thick juice. For a thin drink, mix with mineral water as instructed here. For a thicker shake, use semi-skimmed milk instead.

½ a mango
½ a papaya
1 banana
75–100ml (3-4 fl. oz) sparkling mineral water
3–4 cubes of ice

Peel the mango, slice the fruit off the stone and cut the flesh into chunks. Cut the skin thinly from the papaya, remove the seeds and cut the flesh into pieces. Peel the banana and cut into chunks. Put all the ingredients into the blender and whiz until smooth.

Kiwi Krush

Kiwis add lots of vitamin E to this delicious vitamin power drink. The pineapple should give enough sweetness but add a little honey if the blend is too sharp.

2 kiwi fruit
2 × 1.25cm (½ inch) slices of pineapple
½ a papaya
75–100ml (3-4 fl oz) freshly squeezed orange juice
3–4 cubes of ice
a pinch of ground cinnamon

Peel the kiwi fruit and cut into pieces. Remove the skin and any eyes from the pineapple and cut the flesh into chunks. Cut the skin from the papaya, remove the seeds and cut the flesh into pieces. Place all the ingredients in the blender and whiz until smooth.

Orange Spice

If you need energy and are trying to fight off a cold or cough, mix the banana's carbohydrate with the vitamin C of the oranges and the homeo -pathic power of the ginger.

1 banana
2 oranges
1.25cm (½ inch) piece of fresh root ginger
75–100ml (3-4 fl oz) soy milk
3–4 cubes of ice

Peel the banana and cut into chunks. Squeeze the juice from the oranges by hand or in a citrus press. Cut the skin from the ginger. Put all the ingredients into the blender and whiz until the ginger and ice have been completely broken up and incorporated into the fruit mix.

Soda Fountain

The soda adds a sparkle to the aromatic sweet-ness of the lychees and grape juice. The pears add fibre and extra vitamins.

2 pears
6 lychees
75ml (3fl oz) soda water
50ml (2fl oz) freshly squeezed grape juice
3–4 cubes of ice

Peel and core the pears and cut into pieces. Peel the lychees and remove the stones. Place all the ingredients in the blender and whiz until smooth

Soda Fountain

Savoury Soups & Sweet Fools

Instead of mixing pulverized vegetables and fruits with mineral water to make juices, or with milk and yoghurt to make smoothies, blend with yoghurt or crème fraîche to create bowlfuls of thicker, creamy cold soups and velvety fools that zing with flavour and burst with goodness.

You don't need a juice extractor for this section – a blender or food processor will pulp all the ingredients.

Above: Guacamole Plus, Opposite: Orange Oats

Cream of the Crop

Although the beetroot loses a little of its nutrient value when cooked, it is still full of goodness and makes a blend that has that recognizable borscht-like flavour.

1 cooked beetroot
2 carrots
1 stick of celery
4–5 tablespoons crème fraîche or fromage frais
salt and pepper
a little freshly squeezed lime juice
1 tablespoon fresh chopped dill

Remove the skin from the beetroot and cut into pieces. Scrub or peel the carrots and cut into pieces. Scrub the celery and cut into chunks. Put the beetroot, carrots, celery, crème fraîche, lime juice, salt and pepper into the blender and whiz until thick and smooth. Spoon into a bowl, mix in the chopped dill and garnish with a whole dill sprig.

Seeing Red

Seeing Red

More than a smoothie, this mix has all the flavours of a summer salad.

1 red pepper
¼ clove garlic
2 spring onions
¼ cucumber
2–3 tablespoons live natural yoghurt
salt and pepper
a small bunch of chives for garnishing

Wash and deseed the red pepper and cut into chunks. Peel the garlic. Cut the root and top from the spring onions and remove any outer leaves. Peel the cucumber and cut the flesh into pieces. Put the pepper, garlic, spring onions, cucumber, salt and pepper and yoghurt into the blender and whiz briefly so that the ingredients just begin to break up. Spoon into a bowl, season to taste and garnish with snipped chives.

Guacamole Plus

Add the whole beansprouts to a blended mixture of vegetables to give crunch and texture.

1 avocado
a handful of rocket leaves
2 tomatoes
a small piece of red chilli
a few sprigs of fresh coriander
a handful of beansprouts
salt and pepper

Peel the avocado, remove the stone and cut the flesh into chunks. Wash the rocket. Wash the tomatoes, cut into quarters and cut away the hard core. Wash and deseed the chilli. Wash the coriander leaves. Wash the beansprouts. Place all the ingredients except the beansprouts in the blender and whiz until thick and smooth. Break the beansprouts into smaller pieces and fold into the thick soup. Spoon into a bowl and garnish with slices of radish or tomato.

Salad Bowl

These lightly flavoured ingredients blend well to make a smooth alternative to a more traditional bowlful of salad.

a handful of watercress
5–6 radishes
2 carrots
4–5 generous tablespoons of live yoghurt
¼ clove of garlic
a small bunch of chives for garnishing
salt and freshly ground black pepper

Wash the watercress. Scrub the radishes and cut off the root. Scrub or peel the carrots and cut off the top and tail. Cut the flesh into chunks. Put all the ingredients into the blender and whiz until smooth. Season to taste, spoon into a bowl and garnish with snipped chives.

Strawberry Nectar

Strawberries combine with almost any other fruit and cleanse the system as well as delivering plenty of nutrients.

1 nectarine
100g (4oz) strawberries
sugar or honey to taste.
2–3 tablespoons crème fraîche

Wash the nectarine, cut in half and remove the stone. Hull and wash the strawberries. Put all the ingredients into the blender and whiz until smooth. Spoon into a bowl or sundae glass and garnish with a fanned strawberry and a mint leaf.

Strawberry Nectar

Ginger Crunch

Cool Cherry Fool

The flavours of cherries and almonds make a wonderful combination and with the smoothness of the yoghurt and the honey, this makes a great lunchtime or evening dessert.

50g (2oz) blanched almonds
225g (8oz) cherries
3–4 teaspoons honey (more or less to taste)
2–3 tablespoons live natural yoghurt

Put the blanched almonds through the grain mill. Wash the cherries, cut in half and remove the stones. Put all the ingredients into the blender and whiz until smooth. Spoon into a bowl and garnish with a couple of whole cherries or some toasted flaked almonds.

Ginger Crunch

This delicious thick soup is full of all sorts of interesting flavours and textures and has the extra iron of the parsley and all the digestive benefits of the root ginger.

1 small cooked beetroot
½ head of fennel
½ an avocado
a few sprigs of parsley
1.25cm (½ inch) piece of fresh root ginger
200–225g (7–8fl oz) crème fraîche or fromage frais
salt and freshly ground black pepper

Cut the skin from the beetroot and cut the flesh into chunks. Wash the fennel and cut away any damaged parts. Cut the flesh into pieces. Cut the skin from the avocado, remove the stone and cut the flesh into pieces. Wash the parsley. Cut the skin from the ginger. Put all the ingredients into the blender and whiz as smooth as possible. Season to taste. Spoon into a serving bowl and garnish with chopped parsley or a sprig of dill.

Tropical Treat

Add the halved grapes to the velvet blend of tropical fruits to make a delicious mixture of crisp sweetness and smooth fool.

1 guava
1 × 1.25cm (½ inch) slice of pineapple
2–3 tablespoons fromage frais
2–3 teaspoons honey
50–75g (2–3oz) red grapes

Cut a thin layer of skin from around the guava and cut the flesh into pieces. Cut the skin and any eyes from the pineapple and cut into chunks. Put the guava, pineapple, fromage frais and honey into the blender and whiz until smooth. Cut the grapes in half and remove any pips. Add to the mixture and stir. Turn into a dish or sundae glass and garnish with a couple of whole grapes.

Orange Oats

This is a great morning mix – fibre, vitamin C, concentrated fruit sugar, protein, minerals and essential fats. Add extra honey for more sweetness, if needed.

3 apricots
1 orange
2–3 tablespoons live natural yoghurt
1–2 tablespoons muesli
a few raisins or sultanas
2 teaspoons toasted sunflower or sesame seeds for garnishing

Wash the apricots, cut in half and remove the stones. Juice the orange by hand or in a citrus press Put the apricots, orange juice, yoghurt, muesli and raisins or sultanas into the blender and whiz until smooth. Turn into a serving dish or sundae glass and garnish with toasted sunflower or sesame seeds.

Autumn Sun

Autumn Sun

This will remind you of picking the shiny berries in late summer or autumn and turning them into crumbles and compôtes with freshly picked juicy apples.

50–75g (2–3oz) blackberries
1 apple
4 teaspoons honey
2–3 tablespoons fromage frais
toasted sunflower or sesame seeds to garnish

Pick over and wash the blackberries. Peel and core the apple and cut into pieces. Put the blackberries, apple, fromage frais and honey into the blender and whiz until smooth. Turn into a bowl or glass and scatter over the toasted sunflower or sesame seeds.

Tropical Treat

Supertonics

Designed for specific occasions and health problems, tonic mixes can be adjusted to suit whatever fruits and vegetables are in season. Use the vitamin and mineral tables in chapter 1 to identify alternative or extra ingredients. If adding the suggested herbal and homeopathic extras, always read instructions on packets and tins carefully. These add-ins are optional and can be added to any blend to suit your personal dietary needs.

To make these mixes, you need a juice extractor, a blender, a citrus press or lemon juicer and a grain mill.

For an extra energizing booster, drink a 25g or 50g (1oz or 2oz) dose of wheatgrass juice as a pre-juice or follow-up shot at your local juice bar.

Above: Pick-You-Up. Opposite: Love Potion

Breakfast Blaster

Breakfast Blaster

Designed to set you up for the morning, this gives a mix of all the essentials, and a dose of acidophilus gives the digestive system the good bacteria it needs to stay healthy.

2 oranges
1 banana
3–4 teaspoons sesame seeds
2 tablespoons muesli
3–4 teaspoons honey
a measure of acidophilus powder – optional

Squeeze the juice from the oranges by hand or in a citrus press. Peel the banana and cut into chunks. Run the sesame seeds through the grain mill. Put the orange juice into the blender with all the other ingredients and whiz until smooth.

Cold Attack

As with all juices made with citrus fruits, this is packed with vitamin C and helps to fight off infections. The ginger helps combat sinus problems or congestion.

1.25cm (½ inch) piece of root ginger
1 lemon
2 oranges
2–3 teaspoons honey
mineral water

Cut the skin from the ginger. Juice the lemon and oranges by hand or in a citrus press. If possible, allow some of the flesh to drain off with the juice. Put the juice and flesh into the blender with the ginger, honey and water and whiz until smooth.

Detox Special

The dandelion and nettle extracts help clean the kidneys while the mix of vegetables stimulates the system to eliminate unwanted toxins.

1 apple
2 sticks of celery
2 carrots
8–10 drops extract of nettle
8–10 drops extract of dandelion

Wash the apple and cut into pieces. Scrub the celery and carrots and cut into chunks. Put the fruit and vegetables through the juice extractor. Add the extract of dandelion and nettle and mix well.

Revitalizer

The vegetables' naturally high sugar content gives energy to combat tiredness and the mix of vitamins replenishes necessary nutrients. Spirulina adds a concentrated burst of antioxidants, vitamins and minerals.

1 beetroot
2 carrots
1 orange
1 measure of spirulina powder – optional

Scrub or peel the beetroot and cut off any root. Cut the flesh into pieces. Scrub the carrots and cut off the root. Cut the flesh into chunks. Juice the orange by hand or in a citrus press. Put the beetroot and carrots through the juice extractor and add the orange juice and spirulina to the extracted juices. Mix thoroughly.

Revitaliser

Morning After

Immune Booster

This mix helps the body fight infections and delivers a concentration of vitamins A, B and C. Echinacea adds a blast of strengthener to the immune system.

1 apple
1.25cm (½ inch) piece of root ginger
2 passion fruits
2 kiwi fruits
a little honey
10 drops echinacea – optional

Wash the apple, cut into pieces and put through the juice extractor. Peel the ginger. Cut the passion fruits in half and scoop out the flesh and seeds. Peel the kiwi fruits and cut the flesh into chunks. Put the apple juice and all the other ingredients into the blender and whiz until smooth.

Morning After

Got a hangover? Pure fruit and vegetable juices like this mix help the body detox and get back its normal balance.

1 medium beetroot
1 apple
1–2 sticks of celery
1 carrot
1 lemon

Peel the beetroot and cut into chunks. Wash the apple and cut into pieces. Scrub the celery and carrot and cut into chunks. Juice the lemon by hand or in a citrus press. Put the beetroot, apple, celery and carrot through the juice extractor, add the lemon juice to the juices and mix well.

Brain Power

The folic acid in the apples and carrots helps keep the brain in good working order while the gingko and brahmi help develop the memory and intelligence.

2 apples
2 carrots
5cm (2 inch) piece of cucumber
a few drops of gingko – optional
a few drops of brahmi extract – optional

Wash the apple and cut into pieces. Scrub the carrots and cut into chunks. Wash the cucumber and cut into chunks. Put the apples, carrots and cucumber through the juice extractor. Add the gingko and brahmi to the extracted juices and mix well.

Pick-You-Up

Echinacea helps the body to heal itself, while the vitamin burst of the fruit promotes the regrowth of body tissues and helps protect from further damage.

2 apples
50–75g (2–3oz) blackcurrants
3–4 teaspoons honey
1.25cm (½ inch) piece of ginger
75–100ml (3–4fl oz) mineral water
10 drops of echinacea – optional

Wash the apples, cut into pieces and put through the juice extractor. Wash the blackcurrants and remove stalks and tails. Cut the skin from the ginger. Put the apple juice and all the other ingredients into the blender and whiz until smooth.

Energy Plus

Carbohydrate and fruit sugar combine to give energy. Sunflower seeds add essential oils, and a dose of spirulina blue-green algae is packed with concentrated proteins, minerals and anti-oxidant vitamins.

1 banana
1 mango
1 tablespoon sunflower seeds
3–4 teaspoons honey
1 measure of spirulina powder – optional

Peel the banana and cut into pieces. Peel the mango and cut the flesh from the stone. Run the sunflower seeds through the grain mill. Put all the ingredients into the blender and whiz until smooth.

Love Potion

An aphrodisiac juice made with grapes – the fruit of Dionysus, Greek god of fertility and procreation, and thought to have stimulating properties – and gingko, which has been used by the Chinese for more than 5,000 years for increasing sexual energy.

½ a papaya
2 × 1.25cm (½ inch) slices of pineapple
50g (2oz) grapes
1 lime
a few drops of gingko

Peel the papaya, remove the seeds and cut the flesh into pieces. Cut the skin from the pineapple and cut into chunks. Wash the grapes. Squeeze the lime juice by hand or in a citrus press. Put the papaya, pineapple and grapes through the juice extractor. Add the lime juice and gingko to the extracted juices and mix well.

Digestion Suggestion

Bee pollen contains enzymes that help the digestive system to function healthily and ginger is good for indigestion and helps to settle the stomach.

2 handfuls of spinach
3 carrots
1.25cm (½ inch) piece root ginger
1–2 teaspoons of bee pollen granules – optional

Wash the spinach. Scrub the carrots and cut off the root. Cut the flesh into pieces. Remove the skin from the ginger. Put the spinach, carrots and ginger through the juice extractor. Add the bee pollen to the extracted juices and stir thoroughly.

Muscle Maker

The carbohydrate content of this blend gives energy while the vitamins help the body fight cell deterioration.

1 grapefruit
1 papaya
50g (2oz) strawberries
2–3 apricots
50–75ml (2–3 fl oz) sparkling mineral water
3–4 cubes of ice

Cut the grapefruit in half and cut the flesh from between the membranes with a curved grapefruit knife or a sharp pointed knife. Remove any pips. Peel the papaya, remove the seeds and cut the flesh into chunks. Hull and wash the strawberries. Wash the apricots and remove the stones. Put the grapefruit flesh, papaya, strawberries, apricots, water and ice into the blender and whiz until smooth. Thin with a little more mineral water if required.

Muscle Maker

Shake it Out

Another mixture to prepare the body for intensive activity – plenty of carbohydrate and natural sugar and the added boost from a favourite protein powder.

1 banana
50g (2oz) raspberries
50g (2oz) blueberries
2 tablespoons live natural yoghurt
3–4 teaspoons honey
protein powder
toasted sesame seeds

Peel the banana and cut into pieces. Pick over and rinse the berries. Put all the ingredients into the blender and whiz until smooth. Garnish with toasted sesame seeds.

Shake It Out

Unwinder

The addition of lemon balm and brahmi to any blend makes a naturally calming drink.

2 carrots
3–4 leaves of lemon balm
2 × 1.25cm (½ inch) slices pineapple
a few drops of brahmi extract – optional

Scrub the carrots, cut off the tops and cut the flesh into chunks. Put the carrot through the juice extractor. Cut the skin and any eyes from the pineapple and cut into pieces. Wash the lemon balm leaves. Put the carrot juice and the other ingredients into the blender and whiz until smooth.

Index

Note: For the nutritional properties and health benefits of each fruit, vegetable, etc. *see* the individual entries.

A

acidophilus 57
alfalfa 13, 15, 41
almonds 13, 14, 53
anise 54
antioxidants 9, 41
Apple Zinger 62
apples 14, 23–4
apricots 12, 24, 59
Autumn Sun 85
avocados 13, 41, 43

B

bananas 13, 14, 24
Banango 75
barleygrass 57
basil 54
beansprouts 12, 43
bee pollen 57
Beet It 62
beetroot 14, 43, 45
Berry Shake 77
The Big Breakfast 75
blackberries 14, 25
blackcurrants 25
blenders 19
   fruit preparation 17, 19
blueberries 25
brahmi 57
Brain Power 91
brazil nuts 14, 53
Breakfast Blaster 88
brewer's yeast 14, 57
broccoli 12, 13, 15, 45

C

C Blast 65
calcium 14, 24, 59
carbohydrates 15
carrots 12, 15, 45–6
cashew nuts 13, 14, 53
celery 13, 14, 15, 46–7

cherries 13, 15, 28
chilli 54
chives 54–5
chromium 14
citrus fruits 15
citrus presses 17, 19–20
Citrus Sensation 77
Cold Attack 88
Cool Cherry Fool 84
coriander 55
cranberries 28
Cranberry Cooler 77
Cream of the Crop 82
Crimson Cleanser 63
cucumbers 47
The Curl 63

D

damiana 57
dandelion 55
dates 14, 59
Detox Special 89
Digestion Suggestion 92
dill 55

E

echinacea 57
Energy Plus 91
enzymes 9, 11
equipment for juicing 17–21

F

fat 15
fennel 15, 47, 55
fibre 15
figs 59
food processors 19
fools 83–5
fruit
   nutritional value 23
   preparation 17, 19, 23
Fruit Punch 66

G

garlic 14, 15, 47

Gerson, Max 7
ginger 55
Ginger Crunch 84
gingko 57
ginseng 58
Go Bananas 73
grains 15, 54
grapefruit 13, 28
grapefruit seed extract 58
grapes 14, 15, 28–30
Guacamole Plus 82
guavas 13, 30

H

hazelnuts 13
herbs 54–5
homeopathic "superfoods" 57–9
honey 59
Immune Booster 90

I

iron 14, 59
Iron Rations 64

J

juice bars 6–7
juice extractors 17, 19, 20–21
   fruit preparation 19
juice squeezers 17, 19
juices
   and disease prevention 7
   history of 6–7
   mixing of 11, 53, 61
   naked 61–8
   nutritional value 7
   raw, benefits of 11
   ready-to-drink 59
juicing
   equipment 17–21
   fruit preparation 17, 19

K

kale 47–8
kiwi fruit 13, 30
Kiwi Krush 78

L

lemon balm 55
lemons 13, 30, 32
lettuces 12, 13, 14, 48
limes 13, 32
liquidizers 19
Love Potion 91
lychees 32

M

magnesium 14
manganese 14
mangoes 12, 13, 32
melons 12, 13, 15, 32
   see also watermelons
milk 12, 13
mineral water 59
minerals 14
mint 55
Morning After 90
Muscle Maker 92

N

nectarines 32, 34
nettle 55
A New Leaf 67
nutrition 9, 11–15
nuts 13, 15, 53

O

oats 14, 54
onions 13, 48
Orange Oats 85
Orange Spice 79
oranges 13, 34
Orchard cream 75
oxidation 9, 17

P

papaya 12, 13, 15, 34
parsley 14, 55
parsnips 14, 48
passion fruit 34
Passion Juice 66

Peach Dream 67
Peach Latte 73
peaches 34, 36
peanuts 13, 14
pears 36
pecan nuts 14, 53
peppers 12, 13, 14, 15, 48–9
phosphorus 14, 59
phytochemicals 9, 11, 15
Pick-You-Up 91
pineapples 13, 14, 15, 36
Pink Passion 77
Pink Perfection 68
plums 15, 36
pomegranates 38
potassium 14, 24
protein 15
protein powders 58
prunes 14, 59
pumpkin seeds 14, 53

R

radishes 14, 15, 49–50
raisins 14, 59
raspberries 14, 15, 38–9
raw juice, benefits of 11
Red Devil 65
Revitalizer 89
rocket 50
Roots 63
rosemary 55

S

Salad Bowl 83
seeds 13, 15, 53
Seeing Red 82
sesame seeds 13, 14, 53
Shake it Out 93
smoothies
   dairy 71–5
   non-dairy 75–9
Soda Fountain 79
soda water 59
soups 81–3, 84
spices 54–5
spinach 13, 14, 50
spirulina 53, 58

strawberries 13, 14, 15, 39
Strawberry Nectar 83
sugars 15
sultanas 59
Summer Fizz 78
sunflower seeds 53
supertonics 87–93

T

tangerines 12
Tangy Avocado 75
thyme 55
tomatoes 12, 13, 15, 50
Tropical Tang 68
Tropical Treat 84

U

Unwinder 93

V

vegetables
   nutritional value 41
   preparation 41
vitamins 9, 12–13, 23
Vitamix 64

W

walnuts 13, 14, 53
watercress 12, 13, 14, 50
watermelons 39
wheatgerm 12, 13, 14, 54
wheatgrass 58

Y

yoghurts 59

The publishers would like to thank the following sources for their
kind permission to reproduce the pictures in this book:

AKG London 5br, 29, 33, 37/Erich Lessing 22, 26-7
Pam Bewley Publicity 18, 19
©Carlton Books Ltd/Howard Shooter
3, 13br, 25, 36, 38, 39t, 46-48, 49b, 50, 54-56, 58-93
Cephas/TOP/Michel Barberousse 21
e.t.archive 45, 48t/Natural History Museum 34b
The Image Bank/Steve Allen 49t, BV & B Productions
5bl, P.E. Berglund 14tr, Anthony Johnson 12bl, L. Wallach 4
Frank Lane Picture Agency/B Borrell 30, 39b, Carpentier/Sunset 13tr,
B.B. Casals 52, Paul Hart 44, E & D Hosking 42-3, Gerard Lacz 24t,
Fritz Polking 34t, Silvestris 57, M J Thomas 40, 51, Larry West 24b
Tony Stone Images/Lori Adamski Peek 8, 10, Thomas Croke 28,
Davies & Starr Inc. 12br, 13cl, 14bl, Donna Day 7, 16, Laurie Evans 35,
Andrea Monikos 12t, Ian O'Leary 5t, Frank Orel 96, Victoria Pearson 20,
Steve Taylor 31, Bob Thomas 6

Every effort has been made to acknowledge correctly and contact the source and/copyright holder
of each picture, and Carlton Books Limited apologises for any unintentional errors or omissions
which will be corrected in future editions of this book.

Juice bars are trendy places to eat, drink and be healthy!